Engage Now International:
I'm Engaged

Disclaimer/Warning:

This book is intended for lecture and entertainment purposes only. The author or publisher does not guarantee that anyone following these steps will be successful in engaging students or employees. The author and publisher shall have neither liability responsibility to anyone with respect to any loss or damage cause, or alleged to be caused, directly or indirectly by the information contained in this book.

I'M ENGAGED

The Ultimate Guide to Recruit, Retain and Reproduce Engaged Students on Campus.

"When you relinquish the core of who you are in pursuit of being like someone else, you give up your ability to make an impact in this world!"

—Mike Fritz

Mike Fritz

Founder and CEO of Engage Now International

Quotes From Mike

"When you relinquish the core of who you are in pursuit of being like someone else, you give up your ability to make an impact in this world!"

"Success happens within your gift-set."

"Recruitment is the foundational element of organizational growth on any campus."

"One of the most powerful ways to grow a leadership team is to leverage the experience and training that has already been invested into your leaders through retention."

"People promote what they create. People support what they help build."

"Engagement is built on the foundation of responsibility."

"Teams that play together stay together."

"A team without a vision will eventually feel lost"

"It is your job as a leader to make sure there is an equipped leader to take over when you leave."

Mike is the ideal Speaker for your next event!

Table of Contents

Table of Contents

Section 3: Reproducing Leaders

Bonus Section
The 5 People Who Walk Your Campus

Engagement Starts with You!

1

Are you a Leader?

"Leadership is influence." —John Maxwell

You don't have to study leadership very long to learn that everyone has his own way to define it. Here are just a few:

"A leader is one that knows the way, goes the way and shows the way." —John Maxwell

"If your actions inspire others to dream more, learn more, do more and become more, you are a leader." —John Quincy Adams

"Great leaders don't set out to be a leader, they set out to make a difference. It's never about the role, it's always about the goal." —Lisa Haisha

"Leadership is about making others better as a result of your presence and making sure that impact lasts in your absence." —Unknown

"The function of leadership is to produce more leaders, not more followers." —Ralph Nadar

"Leadership is the capacity to translate vision into reality."
—**Warren Bennis**

"A true leader has the confidence to stand alone, the courage to make tough decisions and the compassion to listen to the needs of others. He/she does not set out to be a leader, but becomes one by the equality of his actions and the integrity of his intent." —**Douglas McArthur**

"Leadership is about being of service to others, not being served by others. Be a mentor not a boss." —**Unknown**

And one of the most widely accepted leadership quotes available is by John Maxwell:

"Leadership is influence." — **John Maxwell**

In just a cursory search for "leadership definitions" hundreds come up. The word leadership is one of the most widely used words in the human vocabulary and there seems to be thousands of ways to define and describe it.

So what does *Leadership* really mean?

If you look at just the few definitions provided above there is a major common thread to them all. A leader focuses on the wellbeing, growth and success of others.

The number one thing needed to increase student engagement is the increase of leadership on campus. We need you to step up and be more concerned about the wellbeing and growth of others than you are about yourself. I know that sounds a bit harsh, but that is the true essence of leadership.

Here are 3 things that you can do today to increase your ability to lead on campus:

1. Grow Yourself

We as leaders are tasked with working on ourselves constantly. Every day, week, month and year is more time to develop ourselves into the kind of person that can effectively lead others. This may seem like a daunting task but after a while growing and changing is addicting. It gives you the opportunity to literally become the person you want to be.

What are two areas of your life you'd like to change? Would you like to lose some extra weight, work out and get a little bit healthier? Would you like to be able to connect with people faster and build more relationships? Would you like to improve your public speaking skills? What are you working on today that will position you to help others become more successful?

The reason this is important is that leaders are continually growing themselves…PERIOD.

If you aren't actively focusing on something to improve then you most likely aren't growing. If you aren't growing you will soon be passed by those you are entrusted to lead.

1. Read

I didn't read a complete book until after I graduated high school. I hated reading. It's no wonder then that while in high school I was a poor leader. I wasn't growing myself.

As stated above, a leader must be growing themselves continually. Reading is one of the NUMBER ONE ways to identify things in your life you'd like to change and learn practical ways to improve.

At the age of 24, I decided to go to college for the first time, and remember I didn't read a book until after I graduated high school. However, when I enrolled in college I needed to read hundreds of pages per week just to keep up with the demanding class syllabus. What happened? I began to fall in love with reading and now I read 2-4 books a month.

That means that I am being impacted by 24-48 people every year. You can't help but become a better leader when you are learning and growing through reading.

1. Get Wrapped Up *In* The Lives Of People

At the end of the Olympics, the medalists stand on the podium and are awarded for being one of the top 3 competitors in the world in their sport. In looking at this analogy, it isn't the job of the leader to stand on the pedestal so that people look at them and it isn't the job of the leader to help people onto the pedestal; it is the leader's job to BE the podium and allow others to stand on their shoulders and celebrate their efforts. Your role as a leader is serve your team in such a way that they are successful and celebrated by others.

Every time I watch the Olympics I am reminded of this example. I always look at the podium and think to myself "This represents parents who financially invested into their kids, coaches who put everything they had into these athletes, teachers, community workers and friends who all played a role into them getting to where they are."

You must get wrapped up in the lives of others. That means when you are in conversations, you ask more questions than you give answers. You listen to another's story even if you don't get to tell your own. Every conversation then becomes about learning about people so that you can better serve them… because remember: serving others to help them succeed and be celebrated is part of your role as a leader.

Notes

_____

_____

_____

_____

_____

_____

_____

_____

_____

_____

_____

_____

_____

_____

_____

_____

_____

www.EngageNowInt.com

2

The 80/20 Rule

"A winner is someone who recognizes his God-given talents, works his tail off to develop them into skills and uses these skills to accomplish his goals."—**Larry Bird**

Your role in increasing student engagement is directly related to how often you operate in your gift-set. I like to go by the 80/20 rule. 80% of your time should be operating where you are gifted and 20% of your time should be spent in areas that you need to improve.

No matter what organization you are a part of (and if you have not yet become involved in an organization on campus - do so now), your goal is to play a role in that group that highlights your gifts. One of the number one ways to get other people involved in campus organizations (and keep them involved) is to keep them in their area of giftedness as much as possible.

If you have members who are amazing detail-oriented people you want them organizing the details of campus events. If you have people who are gifted in promotion and marketing, you want them promoting your organization and events. If you have people who are great speakers, you want them introducing people at your events. You get the idea.

I just walked away from a company that I was part owner in because the company needed me to operate outside of my gift set too often. I found myself unhappy, unmotivated and feeling unsuccessful. The moment I walked away and started getting back to the roots of my true passion and gift-set I felt a rush go through my heart.

While I was running this company I was working on spreadsheets, business administration, customer service, and the many other tasks involved in the administration of a business. When I spent time on these things it took time away from where I could really add value to people: speaking, marketing and business coaching. Those are the areas where my giftedness is clear.

"Success happens within your gift-set." —**Mike Fritz**

Notes

_____

_____

_____

_____

_____

_____

_____

_____

_____

_____

_____

_____

_____

_____

_____

_____

_____

_____

3

What would you say into the "Magic Mic"?

One of the things I love to do when speaking to students is an exercise that I call the "Magic Mic". The goal of the exercise is to get at the heart of peoples' passions and goals.

Here's how it works: I tell the students, "If I were to hold in my hand a microphone that had the power to reach the entire world, and anytime you speak your message into this microphone the entire world would hear. You would have everyone captive in a moment to simply listen to what you had to say, but you can only take 10 seconds to share your message. What would you say?"

It is amazing to hear the passion and motivation of people and their desire to make the world a better place. I have heard people say things like:

"You are beautiful no matter what people have told you."

"You can reach any goal you want if you just believe."

"You are a masterpiece."

"Nothing is impossible for people who have the desire and dedication to succeed."

These messages may sound trite but imagine if the right person heard them. The person who has been told his or her whole life that he or she isn't good enough and now hears that s/he indeed is good enough; or the person who feels completely ugly is told they are beautiful. This can literally change people's lives.

There are 2 pitfalls to watch out for when adopting this powerful concept. One is to think that words are all-powerful, meaning all you have to do is speak it and it will be accomplished. The other is to think that words have no power and you never speak your true desires and passions. Words without actions are crippled, but so are actions without words.

This exercise is so near and dear to me because I want students to get used to sharing their message with the world and dreaming big. But this has a HUGE implication on student involvement and engagement.

It is only when the "already involved" students are pushing what they believe in and are passionate about, that the masses will get excited enough to get involved and start playing a role in the what happens on campus.

Notes

4

Be Weird

What we don't need more of in this world is "normal people". We need people who are willing to be exactly who they are in all their weirdness, craziness and uniqueness.

When I was younger, I had a nickname that I absolutely hated - it was *Spaz*.

I hated it for a few reasons. I was such a crazy kid and always had so much energy that I was put on medication. This lasted until I was in high school. That means that every day as a freshman I had to go and see the school nurse to get my "I'm screwed up" medication (at least that's how I saw it). Because of this I began to hate how I was built and ultimately who I was. I felt like I was a freak who was different than everyone else. It turns out, thank God, I was!

Maybe you can relate. Have you ever gotten up in the morning, looked into the mirror and wished you saw something different? Maybe you wished you were taller, more muscular, thinner, built with different measurements, richer, a different color, smarter etc.

One the biggest struggles of students (and adults) is the issue of identity. Who are you? What do you value? What are your *natural* talents? Most people spend their entire lives trying to be like other people so that they are "accepted" and "celebrated". The problem with this is the only time you are truly accepted and celebrated is when you fully embrace who you are!

Growing up I learned to hate the excess energy I had and the fact that people were trying to medicate it out of me; but something extraordinary happened when I turned 31 years old. This was the age when I realized I had been trying to be someone else and it wasn't working.

I was speaking to a group of students at a local school and someone said to me after I spoke "Man, I can tell you were built for this. The students loved you; and, you had great energy". Wait…could the "energy" I had been given be the very thing that positioned me to make a difference in the lives of students around the world? It turns out, that's exactly what happened!

That's when I wrote my first book "Great Student Leaders Aren't Born, They're Made," launched my full time speaking business and started to travel the country. I found that I was built for the stage. In fact it is the "extra" energy I bring to the stage today that allows me to entertain students across the country and world.

What I once hated is now what sets me apart and allows me to help people in a way others can't.

"When you relinquish the core of who you are in pursuit of being like someone else, you give up your ability to make an impact in this world!"—**Mike Fritz**

People are walking your campus right now looking for a place to belong - a place that will accept them for who they are. If you want to engage students all over your campus, create an environment where students can come and simply be exactly who they were built to be!

1. What is unique about you that gives you a greater ability to impact people?

2. What have you experienced in your life that will help you help others?

3. When are you most prone to envy someone else's life and how can you combat that?

Notes

5

Your Circle of Influence

According to studies done over a decade ago by the late Jim Rohn, a personal development and business philosopher, your income will be the average of the 5 people you hang around most. This is also true of your character. If you want to be a man or woman of great integrity, find a group of people that have amazing integrity. If you want to make more money while in college, hang out with people who earn a lot of money. If you want to be a goal setter and a goal getter hang out with people who set and achieve goals on a regular basis.

I have learned that one of the most powerful things you can do as a leader is to be the person who has the most growing to do in every room, meaning surrounding yourself with others that have mastered what you are seeking to develop and learn. What will happen is sooner or later you will run out of rooms. The circle of friends (and influencers) that you choose to spend time with will directly impact the amount of success you can achieve while on campus, and even the kind of job you can get.

The 5 people that you spend the most time with can essentially determine the trajectory of your life. That being said, the better your circle of influence, the more impact you'll be able to have on those who walk your campus every day.

We all want to follow people who are following their dreams and making a difference. The best way for you to do that is to build a circle of friends who push you to be better. Imagine if the leaders of campus organizations were all working toward being their best and accomplishing their goals together. It is absolutely amazing to be in a group where people aren't worried about competing, but rather are thinking about helping others be successful.

I lead a group of speakers and business owners that are extremely high achievers. Each of the speakers in this group is paid to speak over 100 times per year, meaning they are in the top 1% of speakers earning over 1/4 million dollars a year just from speaking fees. When I come away from these meetings I feel so invigorated.

It may be difficult to see the correlation to your building a solid circle of friends and student engagement; but people want to be a part of groups that are more interested in serving each other than they are in taking from each other. The more you can build a group of people that focuses on helping others become successful the more people will want to join that group.

Notes

_____

_____

_____

_____

_____

_____

_____

_____

_____

_____

_____

_____

_____

_____

_____

_____

Section 1

Recruitment

"Recruitment is the foundational element of
organizational growth on any campus."

—Mike Fritz

1

Recruitment Tip #1
Never Stop Recruiting (#NSR)

One of the biggest mistakes that most companies make is inconsistent marketing. Many times when businesses are doing really well they back off on marketing because it seems as if they don't need it, forgetting that it was, in fact, marketing that got them there in the first place. Other times when companies are struggling and budgets are tight, marketing is often the first place they seek to save, again forgetting that marketing is the only action that creates money in a business. There is no greater parallel to recruiting for your clubs and organizations.

There is NEVER a time where backing off on recruitment makes sense...EVER...EVER...EVER! Sometimes organizations back off recruitment at the end of the year or semester forgetting that the future health of the organization depends on that crucial time of recruitment. I know you may not think of yourself this way, however, when you are a leader in a club or organization you are a marketer/promoter.

One of the most important jobs you have is to continually keep your organization in front of other students on campus. There is a topic in marketing that business owners talk about called "TOMA". It stands for Top of Mind Awareness. The idea here is when people buy a product or service they often buy what is right in front of them, or who they remember most vividly. The same is true of your clubs and organizations. You want people to be exposed to who you are and what you do continually so when they decide to get involved and engaged they remember you!

Most clubs and organizations meet either once a week or once a month. I would definitely advocate for weekly meetings. Weekly meetings give you the opportunity to make changes each week to keep organizations moving in the right direction; not to mention it keeps the objectives of the organization in the minds of its members. Just as TOMA applies to those not involved in your organization it also applies to those within your organization. You want recruitment and the overall health of the organization on the minds of your members constantly. Weekly meetings make this a bit easier.

As you host (or implement) your weekly meetings, recruitment should be something that is discussed every week, no matter what. It would be great to see your club discussing how your current forms of recruitment are working, and if it isn't, then you could brainstorm new ways to reach out to those on campus and get them involved.

One of the reasons that I love speaking on campuses and giving trainings on recruitment is that it gives you, those in your organization, and other club and organizational leaders someone to bounce ideas off as well as acquire some new skills and fresh ideas for recruitment.

[If you'd like to have one of our programs on your campus go to www.EngageNowInt.com and fill out the booking form. I'd love to meet you and your organization.]

Notes

2

Recruitment Tip #2
Presence at as Many Events
as Possible

One of the most powerful engagement tools you have on campus is the events that you create and produce. This is often the first taste students get of what it might look like to get engaged and become a part of something powerful on campus. As stated earlier, you are most likely going to find the people who want to get engaged in attendance at your events.

Whether you have 10, 40, 100 (or more) clubs on campus all of them should be encouraged to put their club and organization on display at events on campus. I often mentioned to the clubs and organizations when I am speaking on campus that they should have a booth at every event that is available for them to do so. Once again, you want to make sure that clubs and organizations are in front of as many people as possible, as many times as possible throughout the year. This is where TOMA comes in. You want to continually have your club in the minds of those who may be potential members.

5 Tips For Exhibiting and Promoting at Campus Events

1. Clear Message

When people walk by your booth or see you wearing a particular t-shirt or grab a piece of your promotional material make sure the message and essence of your club or organization is perfectly clear. You want people to know who you are and what you do as fast as possible. For example if you were to walk by and see a club that said "The Cheese Club" (which is a real club) you would certainly have some questions. Even if you have a fun club like that make sure people know what your club does to embody its mission.

If this is a club for true cheese connoisseurs and the goal is create amazing social events around cheese sampling make sure that is clear in your marketing. You are really a club that connects people using the power of cheese. So if you call it "The Cheese Club" have a tag line that says "Meet new people…make new friends…have fun…AND OF COURSE CHEESE". This lets people know what you're about.

1. Represent Your Club or Organization Well

When marketing your club, represent yourself well visually, vocally and virally. When you have a booth at an event make sure you don't just have a table with no table skirt and some post cards to hand out. This makes your club not only look disorganized, but it gives people the impression that your club just throws things together with little effort or thought (even if this isn't the case).

You want people to see photos, well thought out banners, flyers to hand out, a table skirt with your club on it, etc. This doesn't mean if you don't have all this stuff don't promote your club or organization; it simply means get as much as a you can with the time and budget you have and then keep working toward a really good representation of yourself when people see you. First impressions really are hard to change.

1. Be in a High Traffic Area of the Event

You want your club or organization to be in the highest traffic area of the event that the people throwing the event will allow. You have heard it said in marketing that the three most important things are "Location, Location, Location." While there is certainly more to marketing than this, location is a very important element. If you are marketing your club in a part of the event where most people aren't going to go you seriously limit yourself in the number of people that can be exposed to you and your club's mission.

This may seem like a small detail, but believe me: it is extremely important. You may run into a club or organization that doesn't want booths put right in the middle of where the event is happening, but you want it as close to the majority of the foot traffic as possible.

1. Have Something Students Can Walk Away With

Make sure you have something that they can take back with them, not only to remind them of the opportunity to get involved, but to have something that clearly lays out all the benefits and opportunities of the organization. I would place all of this on no more than one piece of paper (front and back). I like the 6x9 post card size for this piece of marketing even better.

You want to think about this as a piece of marketing. When they walk away with this they may still be contemplating whether or not to get involved. But with all the benefits and opportunities listed on the postcard (or whatever you choose) you may still be persuading them even when they are no longer standing and talking with you face to face.

On this piece of marketing there are a number of things that need to be included: (1) The title of the club or organization and the tag line that embodies the mission of your group. (2) An exhaustive list of benefits they will receive by joining. (3) Testimonials of other students who have been involved in your group and the great experience they had. (4) Pictures of your group having fun doing whatever your club or organization does.

1. Ethical Bribe for Contact Information

One of the most important things you get while meeting people at events is their contact information. When people walk up to your booth it helps to have a drawing or giveaway that requires them to provide you with contact information. Even if they don't win you can contact them and let them know of your club events as well as ask them if they'd like to join your club or organization and become a member. When you get contact information you want to reach out strategically and not bombard them with notifications.

Notes

_____

_____

_____

_____

_____

_____

_____

_____

_____

_____

_____

_____

_____

_____

_____

_____

_____

_____

_____

_____

3

Recruitment Tip #3
People Connect to a Mission
Not a Club

No matter what club or organization you are part of or passionate about, recruiting people to join has a lot to do with the mission you project. People are much more inclined to join a mission rather than an organization. The Red Cross is a humanitarian organization that provides emergency assistance, disaster relief and education in the United States. Now are you inclined to support their mission? The truth is until you know how they do that (their mission) people aren't as passionate to provide support. But when Hurricane Harvey hit Houston they raised millions of dollars to do just that—bring disaster relief. People certainly got on board with the mission "Restore Houston" rather than just "Please help us bring disaster relief to people." When people saw the mission they hopped on board.

As I write this book our country is experiencing massive hurricanes hitting our coasts. One city in particular that has been devastated is Houston. Let's say that I have a passion to make a difference in the city of Houston and I continually sought to enlist people to make a difference in Houston just because we want to make a difference before the hurricane. You will have less buy in than if you were to put together a disaster relief team after a devastating hurricane to bring help and food to hurting people. You see the difference? One is certainly powerful, but the other is one that, literally, millions of people responded to. One is a passion, the other is a mission.

No matter what club or organization you are a part of you most likely have a passion for it; however, if you can translate that into a mission people are much more likely to join. One of the exercises you and your club should go through at the beginning of the year is how you can attach the passion of your organization to a mission that people would love to be a part of.

If your club or organization is Student Activities, you don't produce events - you create experiences for people to meet new people and belong. That has an entirely different connotation.

If your club or organization is an International Students club you don't create a get together - you give international students a place to plug in and find acceptance. Now that's a mission!

If your club or organization is Student Government and you've been voted in to a particular role of leadership you don't "govern student life"…you give students on campus a voice and give clubs and organizations resources to succeed.

If I were a club leader I would love to have a group of people that provided me with resources to succeed. What an amazing opportunity.

I could go on and on but you can see each organization needs a higher mission - one that calls students on the fringes to stand up and join the group designed to make a change... destined to make a difference. People want their life to count. You are giving them that opportunity.

No matter the club or organization that you are a part of I want you to start seeing yourself as someone who changes the game; someone who gives people the ability to belong in the pursuit of making a difference. You are not an organizational leader, you are an "agent of positive change" as my friend Eric Lambert (Founder and president of APCA) says.

Notes

4

Recruitment Tip #4
Run Your Club or Organization
Like a Business

The number one job of every company is to get and keep customers. You'll see throughout this section how running a club or organization is like running a business. If I had to choose one reason why most clubs and organizations fail it is because they miss this point. It can change everything for you and your organization if you apply these principles.

In all the companies that I own (and have previously owned) there are many common denominators.

For example:

1. **Brand** – In any company you need a memorable, sellable brand that communicates the message of your business quickly.

2. **Ideal Client** – You need what we call in the business world "an Avatar". This is a description of your ideal client and the person that is most likely to buy our product of service.

3. **Marketing Plan** – A clear, consistent and disciplined marketing plan is essential to growing and surviving as a company.

4. **Good Leadership** – A company will only succeed when it has someone that knows the value of its team, employees and customers.

5. **Customer Service** – The people who have already become customers need to be taken care of so they refer you and speak well of you in the marketplace.

There is certainly more to running a business, but these 6 things are of paramount value when seeking to launch, grow and expand a company so that it is helping the maximum amount of people and earning the maximum amount of revenue.

I will walk you through these 6 elements to running a successful business and you'll see how much over-lap there is to operating a healthy organization on your campus.

Brand

In business, a brand is your company's promise to the world. On campus your "organizational brand" is your promise to your campus. You will set your club or organization apart by simply branding it. Branding your club can be as easy as having a logo and tagline that explains what you do and the benefit to being a part. For example:

Campus Activities Board (CAB): Creating Unforgettable Experience On Campus

Student Government: Giving EVERY Student A Voice.

National Club Basketball Association: Creating Greatness In Student Athletes.

Health and Wellness (H&W): Giving Every Student The Chance at Optimal Health

As you can see having a brand lets people know what you do and more importantly the benefit of being involved. It is extremely valuable to take your club or organization through this exercise.

Ideal Client

When any business is launching a product or service they ask themselves "Who is most likely to want and buy what we have?" This is the same question you need to ask yourself as a club or organizational leader: "Who is most likely to WANT to join our club or organization?" Is our club more geared toward men or women? What interests would someone who wanted to join our club have?" If it is a political organization, is it more geared to democrats or republicans, or a third party? Would people going after a certain major be attracted to your club?

The reason you put yourself through this exercise is to help with recruitment and marketing. You can target your marketing to a more specific crowd if you have answered these questions. You may be thinking that you have a club that is geared toward all students. I totally understand. The goal isn't to necessarily exclude people, but rather focus on the people that are most likely to desire to join. So your job is to answer as many of these questions as you can.

Marketing Plan

A business without a marketing plan will soon find itself out of business for sure. It is the same way with any club or organization. If you aren't marketing your club and letting people know who you are, what you do and how they can get involved you will soon find yourself asking the question "Should I just throw in the towel?"

Oftentimes when clubs aren't growing it is simply because they aren't consistently marketing and recruiting members with a clear, disciplined marketing plan that keeps their organization's mission in front of their avatar students. Many times a small club is not small because there is no interest; it is small because there is no marketing.

Good Leadership

Everything rises and falls on leadership - both success and failure. When things are going well it's because of great leaders; when things are struggling it's because there are some areas in the leadership that need to be improved. Leadership is the beginning and the end of success. When you want to grow or expand your club or organization you must first ask who/what do our leaders need to become to make that happen.

Leadership is a VERY broad word. It's assembling, training and mobilizing a team in a single direction for the good and benefit of others. People spend their entire lives learning how to be effective leaders in their jobs, business and life. This is why it is so imperative that you and your team understand the way up the ladder of success is to continue to focus on developing the skills that great leaders have mastered over the years.

The 5 greatest things to focus on as a leader are discipline, interpersonal communication, trust, courage and public speaking. In your pursuit of growing in your ability to lead, these are a great place to start This list is not exhaustive; however this is a list that will set you apart as a premier leader on campus and in life.

Customer Service

When you own a business, focusing on getting customers is extremely important, but as important, if not more important, is keeping the customers that you already have. This is done by taking care of your customers and letting them know they are the reason you do what you do. This is how you want to think about your club or organizational members.

You want to serve both your club leaders and your club members relentlessly. If you are hosting an event you want the people who attend to know that they are the reasons that you do what you do! Letting them know that people matter - and more importantly that they matter - to the success of your organization will not only make them want to stay involved longer, but they will have amazing things to say about your group when conversing with others.

If you run your club like a business you will see massive growth and have the opportunity to grow your impact far beyond what you could ever imagine.

[If you'd like to have one of our programs on your campus go to www.EngageNowInt.com and fill out the booking form. I'd love to meet you and your organization.]

Notes

5

Recruitment Tip #5
Why People Do What They Do

The question that has become the obsession of many personal development and leadership gurus over the years is "Why do people do what they do?" The reason this question has literally launched an entire industry is because if this question can be answered, then we have a major advantage to helping people get to where they want to be and get "unstuck" from the things that hold them back.

Why is this important to you?

When you realize why people do what they do, you will have a better understanding why some people want to join your club or organization and why some don't. This information can direct your marketing as well as the brand and message that you communicate to your campus about what your organizations' mission is. It may be a bit fuzzy right now, so let me explain.

According to years and years of research we've basically seen across the board that humans only do things for 2 reasons:

to avoid paid or gain pleasure. It's also important to note that we will do more to avoid pain than gain pleasure. You can track every decision you've ever made back to this paradigm.

It doesn't matter if you're talking about students engaging on campus, employees engaging at work or children following the lead of their parents. If you study child development there are hundreds of methods parents use to discipline and reward their children. Why does a parent tells a child "If you play in the road you will get a time out" or "If you don't clean your room you aren't going to be able to go out and play"? Parents are seeking to associate pain to children not doing what's best for them. Or maybe you've seen parents give rewards to their children for good grades; once again they are seeking get their children to associate pleasure with doing the right thing.

This is one of the most fundamental truths of human existence.

Now think about this in relationship to marketing and leading your club or organization. Students are going to get involved based on their perception of the pain that they believe will experience for not getting involved and the pleasure they believe will be received for joining. So you want to ask this question: "What do college students want?" You want to connect getting involved to what they want as much as possible, as well as help them see what they will miss by passing up the opportunity to get involved.

Things that are often hard for students to get their hands on are time, money, meaningful relationships, etc. These are the things that you want tied to joining your organizations so that students want to be involved. Meaningful relationships are a great one because being a part of a club gives great opportunity for this. Money can be tied to involvement because being part of clubs looks great on a resume - it shows initiative and leadership abilities.

It doesn't matter if you're seeking to encourage people to attend one of your events (check out my book, "How to Double and EVEN Triple the Size of Your Next Campus Event" on Amazon), join your organization or take a leadership role in your mission; you must help them visualize the pleasure that will come with joining the mission and the pain that will be experienced by simply doing nothing.

Notes

Section 2

Retention

"One of the most powerful ways to grow a leadership team is to leverage the experience and training that has already been invested into your leaders through retention."

—Mike Fritz

1

Retention Tip #1
People Engage with Passion
Not Tasks

Once you have done the hard work to recruit top-notch leaders to your club or organization, how do you keep them engaged and involved? When the year is up will they stay engaged over the summer? Will they come back next year with a renewed vision and passion to further the mission or are you going to start each year at ground zero and have to rebuild from the ground up?

The easiest form of recruitment is to hold on to the leaders you had last year, assuming they are still on campus. Don't miss out on the people who are already in your group and committed to searching for new people. The people who are already engaged are your most valuable people on campus in relationship to your organization.

But what is it that keeps people on fire from year to year inside a club or organization?

This question is an awesome and life changing question for you and your club. Your mission is too important to lose steam and momentum from year to year. You and your members, however, are the only hope to gain and maintain momentum.

After speaking to over 150,000 students on campuses across the country I have learned that people engage with what they are passionate about far above the tasks that they are assigned inside the club or organization. In fact, if tasks aren't continually tied to the bigger vision you have busy, but unguided people. This is often where passion starts to wane and people start thinking to themselves "You know…I joined to make a difference, but it just seems like I am planning events".

Remember your mission is the greatest glue to retain people throughout the year and from year to year. Help people see that planning the events, or recruiting and talking to another advisor to see if we can promote our club at their event are part of a bigger picture, larger mission and to ultimately make a bigger difference. Help everyone see how his or her tasks tie to the mission.

Going to the store to buy gallons of water seems like a meaningless task, until it's tied to the fact we are taking it to people who are suffering and could desperately use water. You see, every task that makes a club or organization tick is tied to a much larger and more powerful mission.

Notes

2

Retention Tip #2
People Think About
Themselves First

If you were to ask me what my greatest pet peeve is, it would be people who talk about themselves all the time and don't ask questions of others to inquire and learn about them. I literally can tell if I want to go into business with someone, if I want them on my leadership team or even if I want to spend time with them based on this premise. Your job as a leader is to serve others, learn about others and ultimately your success is measure by the success of others.

While I believe to be self-absorbed is a major character and leadership flaw, we are designed to think about our well-being first. It's been said that everyone wakes up in the morning and tunes into the radio station WIIFM - **What's In It For Me?** It can take quite a while to train this idea out of our DNA. But what if this isn't all bad? What if this is built within us because it gives us the greatest opportunity to help people?

The desire to protect and serve ourselves first, if unchecked, can make us a self-absorbed, small-minded and crippled leader. But utilized correctly, it can make you a powerhouse as a leader. Let me explain.

To lead others successfully you must first develop your own leadership skills. To be a great husband or wife you must first work on yourself as a person. To be able to give and serve others financially you must first earn the money to do so. To help people with their business you must first run a successful business yourself. And the list goes on and on. Thinking about yourself first is the foundation to serving and helping others. You must fill your own tank before you can give others a ride.

Because of this universal truth people look at every situation with biased eyes thinking, "How will this impact me?" before they ever think about how it will impact others. This being said, remember that in marketing and promoting your club or organization, you must focus on the benefits that potential club members will experience by becoming a part of your group.

People naturally respond first to what will benefit them most. People make decisions based on emotions and then justify them based on logic, even when people make a big purchase like a car or a house. The often will buy something they want even if it is out of their price range and then find a justification for it logically saying "Well…we really did need the extra space." This is how humans work, period. Maybe you decided to go to a college because that's where your girlfriend/boyfriend is going rather than what's best for you. We act based on what we want every time.

For every poster you hang or email you send or booth you decorate to promote your club or organization, remember people act based on what will benefit them.

Notes

_____

_____

_____

_____

_____

_____

_____

_____

_____

_____

_____

_____

_____

_____

_____

_____

_____

_____

_____

_____

_____

3

Retention Tip #3
The Quadrant of C.A.R.E.

Nothing will encourage students to remain fired up about a club or organization more than being cared for. The Quadrant of C.A.R.E.™ is a self-review system to evaluate yourself in your pursuit of equipping people who take ownership in their position and their role in your organizations' success.

These 4 elements should be happening continuously. That isn't to say they ALL need to be happening ALL the time, however each one should be a regular occurrence. Can you image what would happen if you implement this system and it started to catch on in your club or organization? And if the people you lead knew beyond the shadow of a doubt that you are looking out for their best interest? Now that would be a great place to be and call "my club"!

The Quadrant of C.A.R.E.™

Connection	Appreciation
The pursuit of what is important to THEM	Demonstrating you are thankful for their hard work in a way that would be meaningful to them
Recognition	Encouragement
Letting others know of the amazing job they are doing	Point out to them what they are doing well

Connection – Making a connection based upon what is important to them

Every person on your team has something that is important to them. For some it could be good grades, finding a significant other, landing their dream job, while for others it could be their family, sports or exercise. Everyone has that thing that when brought up gets their attention, creates conversation and ultimately creates connection.

For me it is my spouse and business. If you get me talking about either of these I can talk for hours. Just the mention of a business deal or taking a vacation with your significant other and I am off to the races. Now imagine knowing that was important to me and being able to connect with me on something that matters to me – which is the only real way to connect with people. You can't connect with people on your terms or with your interests. It's like you telling someone on your team about the recent draft choice of your favorite football team when they don't like football and don't follow your team. Connection isn't about your interests; it's about finding the overlap in interest between you and others. However, if you found out they were into health (like my wife is) talking to them about how to get in better shape would be a great point of connection.

My wife and I are able to connect in a great way over health goals. It is really important to us to live optimally and healthy. We workout regularly, record our foods and caloric intake together and have health goals that we are both striving for.

This is a HUGE game changer. Most students would be thrilled to have a team leader that takes interest in them to that level. Wouldn't it be awesome if you were that person?

Appreciation – Demonstrating you are thankful for your team's hard work in a way that would be meaningful to them.

If I went up to my wife and told her that I was so thankful for all that she did for me that I was going to take her out to an all-expense paid date to Outback Steakhouse and then a movie on Friday night it would not tell her I was thankful at all. You know why? She doesn't like Outback (she is a Raw Foodist) and she doesn't like watching movies; she would rather read. But I love doing both. So, what I was really doing was taking myself out on a date and asking if she'd like to tag along.

The same is true of your fellow students. Each one has a certain way they interpret appreciation, love and care. It is your job to know what that is and deliver appreciation in a way they feel it. You may be saying to yourself "Yeah...but that's not my job" or "Are you actually telling me it is my responsibility to get to know how the people on my team feel appreciated? That will take forever." That is EXACTLY what I am telling you. Too many leaders think they can get the results they want without investing time into their team and showing the appreciation for them that they are looking for. That is a drastic mistake and will most definitely result in decreased loyalty!

[tips on to do this without spending tons of time]

Loyalty is what keeps people going when things get hard. It's what ties people to leaders and a mission. Without loyalty, when obstacles arise people start questioning "why am I doing this?" This can create people walking out at very stressful times in your club and organization. This isn't always the case, but people that are extremely loyal will stick with you no matter the obstacle.

In his book "The 5 Love Languages" Gary Chapman explains this very thing. People interpret appreciation, love and care differently and it is our job as leaders to find out the languages of our team. He offers that there are really 5 ways people receive love: gift giving, quality time, words of affirmation, acts of service (devotion), and physical touch. This is a great resource for student leaders in that it keeps you rooted in the fact that you are dealing with people that have heart beats, problems with self-esteem, their own personal goals, financial struggles...we are working with people, not just students!

Recognition - Letting others know of the amazing job someone else is doing

People reciprocate more when they are made the center of attention and recognition. I know this sounds like I am saying that all people are selfish…but the truth is we are all selfish and that isn't a bad thing. The truth is we all wake up every day and tune in to WIIFM Radio – "What's In It For Me?" This is natural not necessarily egotistical.

Do you think about your grades or your roommates grades? Do you think about your friends more or your roommate's friends? Do you think about the weight that is ruining the health of Sarah from your economics class more often or the 20 extra pounds you need to lose and feel every time you get out of your chair? The truth is we think about ourselves first.

That being said, when people are recognized in front of others for a job well done two things happen: The person being recognized has a sense that they are appreciated, noticed and praised – all of which will create more loyalty and greater effort - and everyone that isn't being recognized asks "What do I need to do to get recognition?" They then have the opportunity to do what it takes to be the next person called out in front of the club meetings for getting great results. It creates a healthy drive to outperform! Why is this true? Because we think about ourselves first – and that's not always a bad thing. You can't give your all if you aren't first taking care of yourself.

Encouragement – Pointing out to someone what they are doing well.

There are 2 ways to motivate people – with fear or encouragement. Both have their place and we will go over this in more detail later, however it must be mentioned here.

Fear is used to motivated people based on what they might lose if they don't perform, encouragement is based on the good things they are already doing and the things they might gain if they perform. If used well, both can be very effective.

When seeking to help someone want to do better than they are currently doing, even if they are performing extremely well, you can either encourage them where they are succeeding which can create a greater desire to push, or point out where they need to improve. Both can work, depending on the situation at hand and the personality of the person you are working with.

Encouragement, however, must be present no matter what path you are taking to drive your team to greater results. People need to know that they are doing a good job. More specifically they need to know that YOU KNOW they are doing a good job.

"Encouragement is the loyalty button of most people; the more you push it they more loyal they become." - Mike Fritz

The point here is to actively look for things that people are doing right and point them out. People love being told that they are doing a good job.

[If you'd like to have one of our programs on your campus go to www.EngageNowInt.com and fill out the booking form. I'd love to meet you and your organization.]

Notes

4

Retention Tip #4
The Power of Collaboration

"Collaboration isn't about being best friends, or even necessarily liking everyone you're working with. It is about putting all and any baggage aside, bringing your best self to the table, and focusing on the common goal."
—**Forbes Magazine**

When working with a team, collaboration is quite possibly one of the most important elements of success. When all leadership cylinders are firing in the same direction teams can accomplish anything they set their mind and intention to. The sad truth is that most teams suffer from a lack of collaboration and trip over egos, hidden agendas and the politics that surround it all rather than a relentless pursuit of a common goal.

First let me make a distinction between cooperation and collaboration. Cooperation is me dealing with the differences and moving forward anyway, while collaboration is team members putting aside individual agendas and working toward a common goal together. Collaboration values consensus not unanimity, meaning we want there to be a general consensus in the group that we are going the right direction rather than everyone voting for the exact same thing. The truth is if your team is 4-12 people it is going to be VERY rare that everyone wants the exact same thing, no matter what you are "voting" on.

One of the key principles of collaboration is that I spend more time and energy seeking to understand where others are coming from rather than defending my position and seeking to be seen as "right." Maybe you have experienced this. When you are in a debate or argument where two parties disagree and when one person is giving her argument the person on the opposing side isn't even listening but instead is mentally formulating a response. So it really isn't a discussion or debate, it is simply people seeking to get people to hear things from their perspective. Great leaders listen intently to their team members; this isn't for the purpose of winning them over to their side but for the purpose of reaching consensus and collaboration.

When you're conducting your organizational meetings you want to aim for collaboration - having everyone's voice heard and taken into account and then the group moves towards a decision that keeps you on track to reach a common goal.

Often people will kick against collaboration. Not to say when you mention it they will argue, in fact most people like it on the forefront of the process because they know their voice will be heard. But there are down sides in peoples' minds as well. They often think (but don't say) when something is successful it's hard for me to get the credit deserved for my contribution. We desire to be stars, as long as there is only one star in the sky.

It isn't wrong to desire recognition for your contribution, but successful clubs and organizations as a group have a greater desire to make a difference on campus than they do to be personally recognized for making a difference. The truth is the people whose lives you impact don't care who's idea it was but rather that it was done at all.

Notes

5

Retention Tip #5
People Support What They
Help Create

"People promote what they create. People support what they help build."

It doesn't matter if you're talking about your house, your car or your friends; people care more about what's theirs. Why are students more concerned about their own grades rather than yours? Because we take more ownership and are more passionate about what we are invested in and what we've helped create.

This is crucial when thinking about the retention and the buy-in you get from your club and organizational leaders. You will have exponentially more buy-in when the mission statement, goals and objectives are created with your team rather than for you team. I am much more passionate about goals that I took part in selecting rather than goals I was handed and told to go accomplish.

This is where collaboration pops its head up again. The more input and inclusion you can gather in the creation of your club's initiatives, goals and events the more inclusion you will get in the execution of those things and the longer people will remain members. If we are going to retain our club and organizational members and leaders for the long haul they have to buy in to what we are working to accomplish. This is nearly impossible to do if they don't take part in creating the plan from the start.

This isn't to say that students who join midway through the semester with a team that is already up and running won't play an important part but it is to simply say that buy-in creates retention over the long haul.

If your club meets once a week or once a month you should be focusing on getting as much buy-in as possible in your meetings. This is an important element to clearly communicate to your members every time you get together. If they are constantly being reminded that their opinion matters and is valued, it creates an "I'm appreciated" attitude; and when people find places where they feel appreciated they don't like to leave.

The underlying truth of this idea is that people and their options matter and are crucial to the club's success.

When I first began taking on leadership roles, I really struggled with this. I was a pastor working with volunteers (unpaid of course). Volunteers are often the hardest people to work with. A typical meeting for me was to inform our volunteers what was going to happen rather than engaging them in the process of deciding what would happen. Soon the natural effects of this style of leadership started to take hold and people on my team started leaving and the team started getting smaller and smaller and fewer and fewer people were excited to be a part.

I had to start getting new leaders week after week and month after month because the only way to keep a team together when you are a dictatorial leader is to keep finding new people that you can "persuade" to follow your ideas. It is much more effective to lead a team alongside of people rather than from the top down. Even from a young age, we all like being asked rather than told.

One of my greatest detriments as a young, inexperienced and naive leader was loads of passion with no wisdom. Please learn from my mistakes and create something amazing WITH your team. Not only will you get much more buy-in and support but your leaders will remain with you much longer.

[If you'd like to have one of our programs on your campus go to www.EngageNowInt.com and fill out the booking form. I'd love to meet you and your organization.]

Notes

6

Retention Tip #6
Responsibility Keeps Your
Team Engaged

"Engagement is built on the foundation of responsibility."
—Mike Fritz

One of the key principles of engagement is giving people a role. It isn't a coincidence that people who have something the team is counting on them to produce are the most engaged. One of the key roles of a leader is to delegate tasks to ensure everything is completed well and on time. Of course you want to delegate tasks and responsibilities to those that are most likely to produce results; however, people with no role will eventually fade out.

The reason for this is that we all want to feel like we are playing a part, like us being there is making a difference. When people feel like the club could go on without them, soon it will. When people come to meetings and they have nothing to report, nothing to run by the team, nothing to help plan they start asking the questions, "Why do I even go?"

I remember the first student leadership team I was a part of. It was at my church. I was on a team of about 12 leaders who met weekly on Wednesdays and ran a youth group for our students on Sundays. Each week during our meetings I pretty much blanked out because I had very little responsibility on the team. Very little that we went over week to week was dependent on me. Then my wife and I agreed to help spearhead an event for our students. Every week from there on out I was asking questions of the group, requesting help and letting people know what was going on. There is a huge shift in the attention that is given when responsibilities are at your feet and the group is counting on you to come through. This is true of everyone in your club or organization.

Think about the people on your team. What role are they or could they be playing that would give them an opportunity to use their gifts and abilities to help grow and expand the organization on campus? Grappling with this question could be the difference between people remaining engaged for the long haul or being involved for a few months and then moving on.

Notes

7

Retention Tip #7
Have Fun Together

"Teams that play together stay together." —**Mike Fritz**

Nothing creates a bond between people like fun and laughter. It creates memories, the desire to spend more time together and a connection that most don't forget. Teams that exhibit a balance of work and play have a much greater shot at success than the team that is all business OR the team that is ALL play. There must be a balance.

Each month in the midst of the hustle of life you should have a night that is just for your leaders and club members that is meant to do nothing but create a great time for everyone to hang out, get to know each other better and have fun!

As we continue our conversation in this section on how to retain student leaders from month to month and ultimately from year to year we can't forget how much people love to have fun. In fact I wrote an entire book titled Making Leadership F.U.N. which you can find on Amazon. Campuses all over the country brought me in to help their clubs and organizations create a fun culture so that more people desired to get involved!

Think about the amazing place of Disney World. You may love it, hate it or anywhere in between but you can't argue that millions of people every year save up loads of money, pack up all of their kids' stuff - oh and of course the kids themselves - fly to Florida, shuttle to the hotel with all that stuff and spend a ton for one purpose - to create memories and have fun.

Billions of dollars every year is spent on golf equipment, greens fees and apparel just in order to have fun.

People will go into massive debt to get a boat, buy all the gear and go fishing just for fun. Most people don't even really know how to fish well enough to have a blast doing it. But the activity is a blast so that is really irrelevant.

But why?

Because people will pay and sacrifice immensely to have fun. So much so that they don't really see it as a sacrifice.

It is a universal truth of all humanity that people love to have fun. People define fun extremely differently but nonetheless people love being happy. Your team may forget what you asked them to bring to the upcoming meeting, it may slip their mind that they were supposed to tell "so and so" that the meeting time was changed, but they will never forget the night when you all were hanging out laughing so hard that their stomach hurt. We rarely forget when we are extremely happy.

Notes

8

Retention Tip #8
Create a Vision and a
Mission Together

"A team without a vision will eventually feel lost"
—**Mike Fritz**

In our lives we are conditioned to evaluate and respond to what we see and then deduce what those facts mean. Maybe you did the exercise in school where you looked at a picture and were asked, "What do you see?" For some of you, you saw an elderly woman while others of you say the silhouette of a younger woman. What we see will impact the decisions we make every time.

Maybe you have heard it said of a leadership team that you need to create a vision or mission statement or you've been asked if you have a vision or mission statement. I definitely agree that a mission statement is needed. Before we move on we must first distinguish between a mission and a vision. A **vision** is a picture in your mind of what's possible.

A *mission* is a decision which part of that vision to focus on

As you may conclude, you can't have a *mission* without a *vision*. But you can have a *vision* but no *mission*; *we* call these people "dreamers." You may know someone (or may even be one) who has loads of great ideas but no plan to accomplish them.

As mentioned above, our thoughts, attitudes and actions are built on the perceptions and definitions of what we see. Therefore what we choose to see is of utmost importance. Wait…can you really *choose* what you see? ABSOLUTELY!!!

When some students fail a math class they see an epic failure and say to themselves "I've never been good at math". Others may look at the same failing grade and say "I need to get a tutor so I can kick math's butt once and for all. I know I can do this." The same situation created two different responses, because the failing grade was placed in front of two different mindsets. The mindset you have will always impact the way you see the world.

One of the best things you can do before developing a vision or mission statement is to work on your mindset. There are a few things that can strengthen your mindset. First, reading great books to help you see what's possible in your life, the second is the kind of people you spend time with. You want to spend time with people that are always telling you that you can do whatever you put your mind to. The stronger your mindset is, the bigger and more effective your vision will be.

Vision Statement

Think about the picture in which some saw an elderly woman while others saw a young woman. How can two different people looking at the same thing see something different? Because what we already believe about something will dictate how we perceive it.

This can be extremely good news or really bad news when it comes to your club or organization.

Ask yourself these questions: "What's possible for your organization?" "How many people could be involved with in the next 12 months?" "Could the impact of your club or organization get national coverage?" What big goal would support your vision?

How you answer these questions will be determined by what you've chosen to believe up until this point. Do you believe that anything is possible? Do you believe that you can do anything that you put your mind to? I hope so. Because if you want your club to have the most campus awareness of any club in the history of your campus you are going to have to believe different than anyone before you!

The picture that already exists in your mind about what's possible for your club will be the reality you experience. This is why it's extremely important that you create a vision of what's possible *with* your team. It's important that one person's negativity doesn't impact the whole group. But on the flip side if someone thinks that greater things are possible we want the organization exposed to that kind of thinking.

At the beginning of the year you and your team should come up with a vision of what's possible and then a mission statement that will guide your group throughout the year.

Mission Statement

After you have dreamt with your team about what's possible then, as a team, choose what you will focus on throughout the year. Is it going to be the size of your club? Is it going to be a certain amount of money raised for a certain cause?

A mission statement keeps you focused throughout the year and helps you make decisions when there are disagreements on the team. The first question (if it applies) when there is a disagreement is, "Which will help us fulfill our mission statement?" This certainly isn't always a slam dunk but it keeps the entire team focused on the main goal of the organization.

In our next chapter we'll talk about goal setting as a team. This is the natural result of formulating a mission statement.

A vision leads to a mission. A mission leads to goals. Goal leads to a plan. A plan leads to results.

VISION — MISSION — GOALS — PLAN — RESULTS

This diagram is extremely powerful when leading a team to identify a common direction, move in the direction and get results as a result of that direction. When this process is in full effect the issue of retention nearly goes away. People that are this involved in creating this will likely stay!

[If you'd like to have one of our programs on your campus go to www.EngageNowInt.com and fill out the booking form. I'd love to meet you and your organization.]

Notes

www.EngageNowInt.com

9

Retention Tip #9
Create Goals and a Plan as a Team

After you have created a vision and a mission statement as a team it is time to lay out goals for the year and a plan to accomplish them. Once again, this process is to ensure your club or organizations' success while creating maximum buy-in from your team members to retain them from year to year until they graduate.

As in the last chapter we saw a difference between a vision and mission statement; it is the same with setting goals and creating a plan.

A *goal* is a point of measurement in which success can be celebrated.

A *plan* is practical action steps that will lead you to accomplish your goal.

Very few clubs and organizations set goals as a team. This is a major reason why club leaders feel unsuccessful. However some club and organizational leaders do set goals with their team and are positioned for great success. Setting goals, however, is still one step short of creating the greatest amount of success possible in your club. After setting goals you want to select a few actions steps that aligns with each one to get maximum results.

Goals

A goal is a point of measurement at which success can be celebrated, or as some have said "A dream with a deadline." The point of this kind of definition is that it gives you the chance to define success so that you know when to celebrate. If I were to walk up to you and ask "Are you successful?" you might be thinking to yourself "Well that depends on who you ask and how you define success." The truth is, success is defined by setting goals.

What would you like to accomplish this year in your club or organization? Look at the list of goals below and see if any of them resonate:

I want to grow our club and organization by 25% this year.

I want to raise $5,000 toward cancer research before the end of the year.

I want to enlist 3 new leaders for our club this year.

I would like to partner with a local business to further our mission.

I want to write my first book this year.

I want to lose 15 LBS.

I want to run a marathon in the next 10 months.

I want write a song in the next 30 days.

It doesn't matter if your goals are for your organization or are personal, the principles still apply.

After you have created a goal then write down 3 action steps you can take to bring it to fruition. If my goal were to double the size of my campus organization here's how I would lay it out.

Goal: Double The Size of Our Club

Plan

Action Step #1 – Contact our Campus Life/Activities Director to see what events make sense for us put up a booth display

Action Step #2 – Put on an "Organization Awareness" Event where the whole purpose is to have fun, let people know what we do and give them an opportunity to be involved

Action Step #3 – Create posters, t-shirts and other promo materials that will create a greater awareness.

While accomplishing these action steps, I have the exact number in mind that I want to attain from each event. If our club number is currently 20 and I am seeking to get to 40, then in everything I do I am keeping that number in front of me. Every time someone joins I am crossing off another number.....

As you can see the goal is the bullseye but the plan helps me aim and hit it. A goal with no plan is really just a dream; and a club with no vision, mission, goal or plan will most likely not see the results it wishes to see.

[If you'd like to have one of our programs on your campus go to www.EngageNowInt.com and fill out the booking form. I'd love to meet you and your organization.]

Notes

10

Retention Tip #10
Operate Inside of Your Gift Set

One of the things that will hinder a club or organization from growth is having people playing a role that doesn't leverage their gift set. This causes them to spend too much of their time doing things that don't come naturally.

I am not a detail person. In fact, I struggle greatly when I have a project to do in which a lot a details are involved. In the business that I run I need a lot of people to handle booking travel, tracking accounts payable, accounts receivable, administration, and more. My strength is casting vision, goal setting, creating an execution plan, marketing and speaking. Any minute I spend outside my natural talents is time wasted.

As I mentioned in the earlier chapter on the **80/20 Rule**, it is best to operate in your gift set 80% of the time and your areas of needed improvement only 20%. Logic says you should spend most of your time developing the weak spots in your leadership and less time on your strengths because those are "already your strengths."

Actually, you should spend most of your time further developing your strengths and do as much as you can to delegate your weaknesses. In your club or organization you want to operate it like a bus stop. At a bus stop, people get off the bus, on the bus and many of them sit in the same seat every time. In your organization you want to get the wrong people off your team, the right people on your team and the people that are on your team on the right "seats on the bus".

The more you can align the roles people are playing with their gift-set the more successful they are going to be and the longer they are going to remain part of the team. People will rarely stick with something that highlights their weaknesses. As a leader your job is to make sure your team feels as successful as possible.

What you do is so important. It would be a tragedy to have your team fail because people are required to do things they struggle with. However, when you are growing a club or organization there are times when everyone needs to pitch in and simply get things done as a team no matter the gift sets of your team members. This is simply a rule of thumb when leading your team. However, when these tasks need to be done the leaders of the club should be the first to step up and serve, not only to set an example, but because that's what leaders do.

Notes

Section 3

Reproducing Leaders

"It is your job as a leader to make sure there is an
equipped leader to take over when you leave."

—Mike Fritz

1

Reproducing Tip #1
Passing on Your Knowledge

Everything you learn as a club or organizational leader is vital to the future of the organization. In every leadership struggle you worked through, late night planning session, meeting that went well and meeting that didn't go so well, you learned things that the future leaders of the organization could greatly benefit from and knowing these things could save them from a ton of growing and learning pains that you have already worked through.

Not all leadership elements have this dynamic, however; club and organizational leadership changes every year. Some students transfer, some students graduate while others just decide to not be involved (review the Retention section). This creates a natural turn over from year to year and can create an up and down effect in relationship to the success of the organization.

What have you learned while being in leadership or being a part of your club or organization?

Have you learned how to deal with difficult people?

Have you learned how to effectively fundraise?

How you learned how to throw a successful event?

Have you learned how to effectively market and promote your club?

Have you learned what events are great to get exposure and what events aren't?

Have you learned how to effectively speak in front of a group?

Have you learned what speakers, trainers and entertainers really connect with students and put on a great event?

Whatever you have learned in your training and time in your club or organization you want to take it with you AND leave it behind by mentoring up-and-coming leaders. The next-year leaders need to know what you did when you had a difficult person on your team, or had an event that no one showed up for, or couldn't get people to pull their weight.

Part of your job as a leader is to successfully hand off the baton to the next person in charge and make sure they have everything they need (that you have the ability to give them) to be successful in the upcoming year. The goal is to pass it along in better shape than it was given to you.

But how do you do that? Great question. The next two chapters will answer that.

Notes

2

Reproducing Tip #2
The Side Car

"Your job as a leader is to reproduce reproducers."
—*Dr. Don McCall*

As stated in the previous chapter one of your roles as a leader is to produce other leaders that are as committed as you and can carry the mission on long after you are off campus and out changing the world in a different way. But how do you do that? The "side car" method is a great way to start.

Maybe you have seen the motorcycles with a side car for a passenger who isn't driving, doesn't have to hold on and is just along for the ride (literally). The side car analogy fits for training leaders who are going to carry the mission forward once you move on.

The side car idea means that you always have someone who is going to be around after you leave doing things with you so they are trained to do your job. You should always be training your replacement. That means when you are executing a contract with a speaker or performer have someone there with you. When you are leading a meeting have someone there with you. When you are speaking in front of a big group introducing someone, have someone there with you. When you are presenting your ideas to the Student Government for funding have someone there with you.

As you can see even the most menial tasks are important to have people alongside of you so that you can continue to impart what you have learned to those who will be executing your leadership functions the following months or years.

The secondary benefit of this to you is that it takes an entirely different skill to train someone to do something than it is to learn to do it yourself. It will develop your leadership skills in an entirely different way. When you apply for jobs, having been involved in after school leadership clubs and organizations is impressive enough, but the fact that you had the wherewithal to think about training the next person to take over for you shows genuine ownership in the mission. This is exactly what employers are looking for in the hiring process. They want to see you thinking like a leader; and thinking about the club after you leave demonstrates great maturity in your leadership skills and overall mindset.

One of the things that you can make sure they don't miss is what you are actually doing with the side car. When you leave and it is their turn to lead you want them looking for the person they are going to take through the side car process so the club and organization can go on strong after they leave, and so on and so on.

This is such a massive leadership shift to make sure your club doesn't take a hit in numbers and effectiveness every time there is a change in leadership.

[If you'd like to have one of our programs on your campus go to www.EngageNowInt.com and fill out the booking form. I'd love to meet you and your organization.]

Notes

www.EngageNowInt.com

3

Reproducing Tip #3
Guided Responsibility

As you institute the side car in your leadership formula one of the best ways to do that is through "guided responsibility". You want leaders to have a chance to practice while still under the protection of someone who knows more than they do and can correct them if need be to make sure something doesn't blow up in their face and leave a bad taste in their mouth for the level of leadership they are stepping into.

As you are guiding him or her to learn the nuances of your leadership role you want to select certain opportunities where they lead but with your guidance. This means they lead the initiative for an event, they lead the meeting, they introduce the speaker or entertainer, they execute the contract with the performer and so on, all with the understanding that you're acting as coach. This gives you the chance to give some great feedback that will help them in the future. We can all be told how to drive, but until we get behind the wheel it's hard to really get a grasp on it. It's the same with leadership. You want your protege to get a chance to lead while still under the protection of your guidance.

After they have given it their best shot and it is time to give some needed feedback there are a couple things you want to remember. People build as much (if not more) on what they did right vs. what they did wrong. It's best to start out identifying things they did well before pointing out areas of improvement. For some reason if people give us 7 things that we did well and 1 thing we need to work on we focus on that 1 thing. So you want to always give a few things they did well, and choose what you have them focus on to improve very carefully. You don't want to have a list of 40 things they "could do better," because they will, most likely, be overwhelmed and may not work on any of them, or they may be so discouraged that they'll disengage.

There are 3 things to remember in this process: first choose the opportunity carefully and make sure you are setting them up to succeed by not choosing too difficult of a first task. Second, choose something that aligns with something they already excel in giving them an opportunity to leverage their gifts. And lastly, chose something that will give them a little bit of challenge to step out of their comfort zone.

[If you'd like to have one of our programs on your campus go to www.EngageNowInt.com and fill out the booking form. I'd love to meet you and your organization.]

Notes

Bonus Section

The 5 People That Walk Your Campus

1

Person #1
The Uninformed and Uninterested

This is the person who doesn't know there are opportunities to get involved and even if they did they don't care, because it just isn't important to them to get involved.

The problem is that organizational leaders often spend loads of time working to convince people they need to be involved in their particular organization. The problem is that you are trying to sell something to someone that doesn't want it. I am not saying that you won't be able to convince some people to get involved, but these people are going to take twice the effort that others will. I'll explain this a bit later.

One of the most important things you will ever learn in organizational recruitment is that going after people that don't want to be involved is a waste of time. You are looking for people who are asking themselves the question "how should I get involved?" not "should I get involved?"

This brings us to a major point of marketing and recruitment: people make decisions to get involved based on what they want, not what they need. You want to spend the majority of your time bringing to the surface of your campus the people who are looking to get involved. We'll go over this a bit later, however it is important to keep this in your mind now!

How can you reach the Uninformed and the Uninterested?

When students are unaware of the opportunities to get involved on campus, and they wouldn't necessarily be interested if they *did* know the best way to engage them is to keep the opportunities in front of them through announcements, posters and organizational marketing.

You don't want to invest loads of time targeting people who aren't necessarily interested in getting involved and engaged. You can bait them, however, with intrigue. You want them to continually see what they are missing by not getting plugged in to your organization.

Due to the fact they don't know that opportunity exists, once they do know, intrigue may take over.

2

Person #2

The Informed and Uninterested

This is the person who knows there are opportunities to get engaged but isn't interested in taking the opportunity to get involved - at least not for now.

This is the person who usually takes the most effort to get involved. If they already know that there are opportunities to get involved have haven't yet because they aren't interested you will be fighting an uphill battle and your time and energy will be better spent focusing on other people on campus.

Many times, already engaged students like yourself ask, "Why don't people want to get involved?" While this is a great question, you are coming from a different frame of reference. One of the things that I would like to warn against is looking at those who aren't involved and judging them as lazy, not wanting to help people, don't get it etc. There are many reasons people aren't interested in getting involved. Our job isn't to judge why, but rather let them know if something changes you'd love to have them on your team of leaders.

How can you reach the Informed and Uninterested?

Once again this group will be reached through general marketing and recruitment. You will spend a lot of time working to convince this crowd to get involved and your time is better spent on those we are going to cover in the upcoming pages.

3

Person #3
The UnInformed and Interested

This is a fun group to work with. They would love to get involved and engaged in an organization if they just knew that they existed, or knew how to get involved. They are looking for a place to belong and start making a difference and they simply need the correct information to do so.

Every time you have an event, the people who show up are more than likely in this category. It takes a certain level of interest to even show up to an event. So one of the best ways to reach out to this group of students is to consistently promote your campus organizations at every event you have. If you have done the hard work in getting people to attend already, capitalize on that effort and let people know how they can get involved.

When it comes to recruitment there is a statement that I say often when I am speaking on campus. It is Never Stop Recruiting (#NSR). Your primary job as a club or organizational leader is to make the mission of your organization known on campus. Remember this group would be interested in getting involved if they just knew there was an opportunity to do so.

This group often has a passion to help people and live a mission-driven life. They really have a desire to make a difference, but haven't quite figured out how to do that yet. This is where you come in. You are going to invite them to join you in your mission to make a difference on and off campus.

How can you reach the Uninformed and Interested?

Make a list of all the events you have going on this semester and invite all of your clubs and organizations to attend and have a booth (it may not make sense at every event) that keeps the opportunity in front of people who are interested.

4

Person #4

The Informed and Interested

This is the best group on campus. They know that opportunity exists and they want to get involved but there is still something holding them back. Usually it is something small; like they don't know who to talk to or they just don't know which club fits them best and need someone like you to help them.

There is still a group of people waiting for someone to invite them to the party. You are going to find this crowd at the events that you host. So everything that applied to the Uninformed and Interested applies here as well. Your best chance to invite them to get involved and engaged will be right after they have made a decision to do so once they attend your event.

There are so many people like this who walk your campus. If someone just invited them they would join. Your clubs, organizations and overall engagement could sky rocket if you just focused on engaging those that were interested in what you have to offer.

5

Person #5

The Committed

This is YOU! These are the people who are already putting their time and freedom on the line to get and stay involved. These are the people who are reading this book. These are the people who are interested in how to get others engaged.

They best thing that you can remember is that you were once one of the 4 people listed above. And you may have even been someone who wasn't really interested in what was happening on campus but someone reached out to you and changed your mind.

The campus will change at the hands of those who are committed...PERIOD! You are the hope for campus engagement. You are the hope to stem the tide and get students involved. You are the hope for students to see campus life as a necessary part to their life. You are the answer...you are the answer...you are the answer!

Conclusion

Those who engage in campus life are not only more likely to get better grades, but are the majority of the alumni donors after they leave school. When you are seeking to grow engagement on campus you are making an investment into the health of the campus that will have effects long after you leave.

But even beyond your impact on campus you are making an investment into people. People are the only thing on this earth that really matter. You are giving people a place to belong and be who they are, a place to serve, a place to make a difference and a place to be a part of something bigger. Every time you feel like your efforts are yielding little to no results remember how important what you do is.

One of my favorite things to do is to join you and your fellow students on campus. I speak all over the country at campuses, just like yours, helping student increase student engagement and leadership skills. Because you have finished this book you are entitled to a 20% discount on my speaking investment to come and speak on your campus.

Colleges and Universities bring me in for welcome week keynotes, student leadership and engagement keynotes and club and organization training where I get to work with all of the club leaders on campus (or just a specific organization).

It would be my pleasure to work with you and your organization on campus or fulfill any of your speaking needs.

You can visit www.EngageNowInt.com to see what programs we offer and what would best fit your campus.

I can't wait to see you on your campus.
Talk soon,
Mike

Take a Look at Mike's Additional Resources

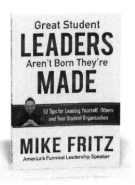

Great Student Leaders Aren't Born They're Made

This is THE leadership book for college students. It provides them with 52 practical ways to start leading on campus immediately. If you are a student leader, parent, teacher, athlete, professor or you are in any other position of influence, this book is for you.

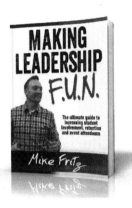

Making Leadership F.U.N.

This is the #1 resource in the world of college leadership books when it comes to getting and keeping students involved in student activities and campus life. With national student involvement on the decline this book is a breath of fresh air and handles the real reason students get involved and stay involved on campus - TO HAVE FUN! This is a non traditional approach to leadership; to the point of excluding people to grow your student organization - yeah you read that right! Don't miss this book that breaks through the "blah... blah" of leadership principles that students have heard a million times and helps club and organizational leaders know what the students that are walking their campuses really want in an organization!

How to Double And EVEN Triple the Size Of Your Next Campus Event

The fear of any college student or coordinator is hosting/ throwing an event only to have a few or no one show up. This books is the answer to make sure that NEVER happens again!!! Get this book, apply its principles and get read for great events with LOADS of people.

Great Teenage Leaders Aren't Born They're Made

If you are looking to become the kind of leader in your school and life that can impact people immediately and leave a legacy in your school, then this is the book for you. It breaks down EXACTLY what you need to hear to become the kind of leader your peers want to follow. This book is your guide to impacting anyone, anywhere, anytime!!!! Go to www.mikefritz.net for more great products.

Rules of Employee Engagement

One of the most important things to master for any manager or leader is how to influence and engage those on your team. Engaged employees boost morale, productivity and ultimately the bottom line for any organization. Leaders have been called to the awesome responsibility of engaging people in the mission of the company and this book gives you a roadmap on how to do just that!

Made in the USA
Columbia, SC
06 September 2020